Fierce Jobs
Air Force Pararescue

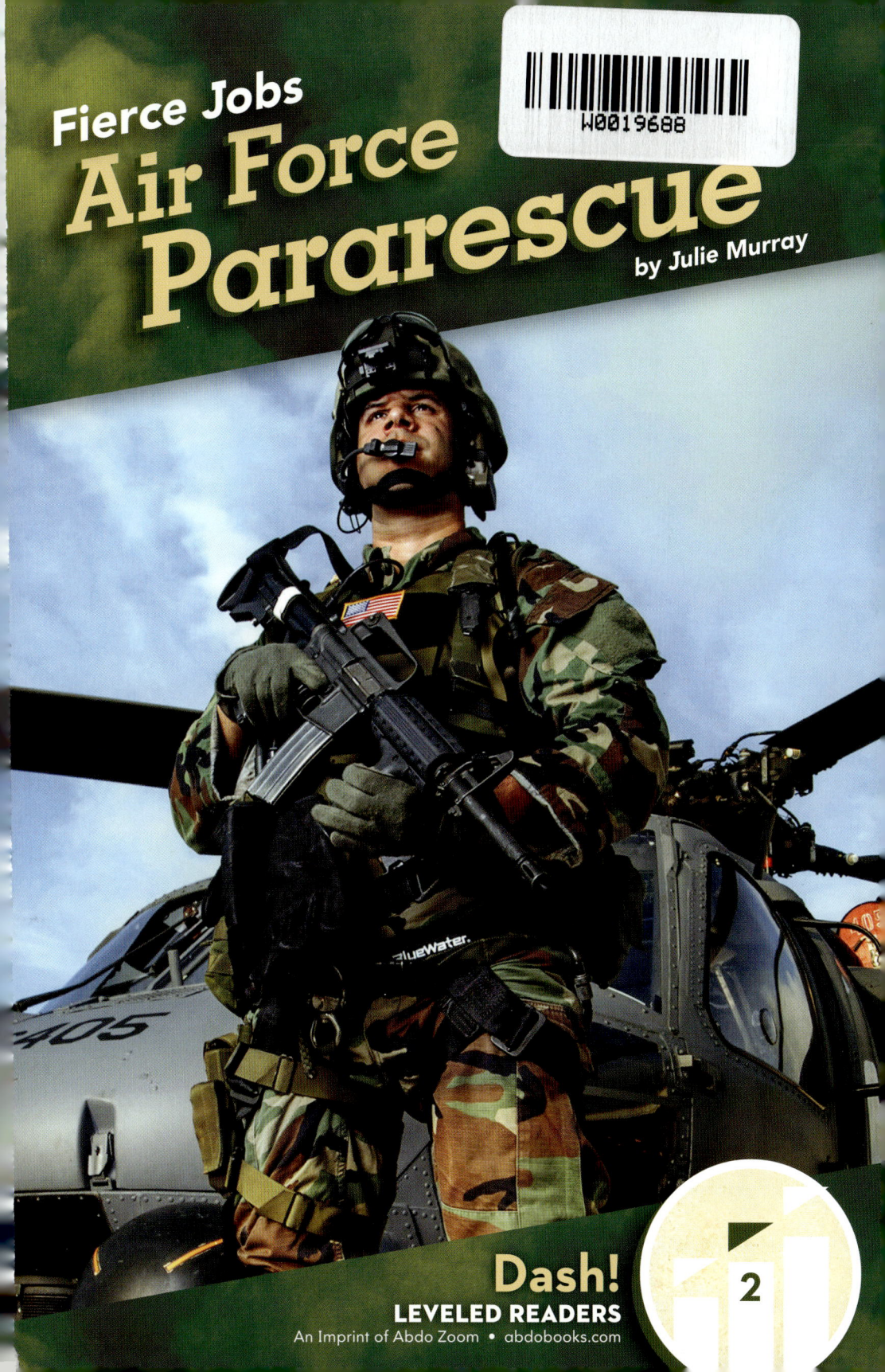

by Julie Murray

Dash!
LEVELED READERS
An Imprint of Abdo Zoom • abdobooks.com

Dash! LEVELED READERS

Level 1 – Beginning
Short and simple sentences with familiar words or patterns for children who are beginning to understand how letters and sounds go together.

Level 2 – Emerging
Longer words and sentences with more complex language patterns for readers who are practicing common words and letter sounds.

Level 3 – Transitional
More developed language and vocabulary for readers who are becoming more independent.

THIS BOOK CONTAINS RECYCLED MATERIALS

abdobooks.com

Published by Abdo Zoom, a division of ABDO, PO Box 398166, Minneapolis, Minnesota 55439. Copyright © 2021 by Abdo Consulting Group, Inc. International copyrights reserved in all countries. No part of this book may be reproduced in any form without written permission from the publisher. Dash!™ is a trademark and logo of Abdo Zoom.

Printed in the United States of America, North Mankato, Minnesota.
052020
092020

Photo Credits: iStock, US Air Force
Production Contributors: Kenny Abdo, Jennie Forsberg, Grace Hansen, John Hansen
Design Contributors: Dorothy Toth, Neil Klinepier, Laura Graphenteen

Library of Congress Control Number: 2019956140

Publisher's Cataloging in Publication Data

Names: Murray, Julie, author.
Title: Air force pararescue / by Julie Murray
Description: Minneapolis, Minnesota : Abdo Zoom, 2021 | Series: Fierce jobs | Includes online resources and index.
Identifiers: ISBN 9781098221089 (lib. bdg.) | ISBN 9781644944035 (pbk.) | ISBN 9781098222062 (ebook) | ISBN 9781098222550 (Read-to-Me ebook)
Subjects: LCSH: United States--Armed Forces--Parachute troops--Juvenile literature. | United States. Air Force--Airmen--Juvenile literature. | Parachute troops--Juvenile literature. | Hazardous occupations--Juvenile literature. | Occupations--Juvenile literature.
Classification: DDC 358.4--dc23

Table of Contents

Air Force Pararescue 4

Training. 12

More Facts 22

Glossary 23

Index 24

Online Resources 24

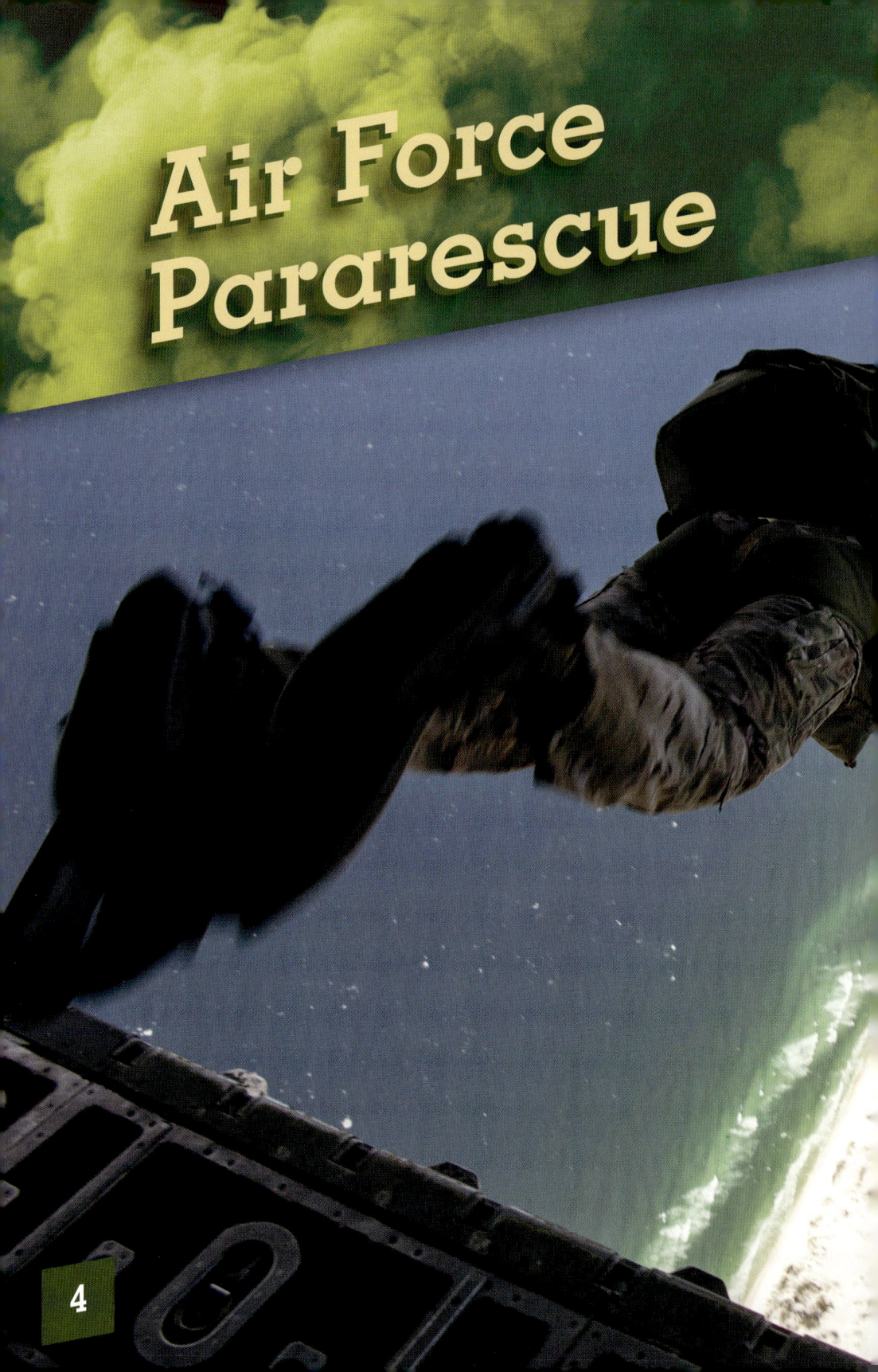

Air Force Pararescue

Pararescue (PJ) specialists are part of the US **Air Force**.

PJs often use parachutes. They jump from planes.

7

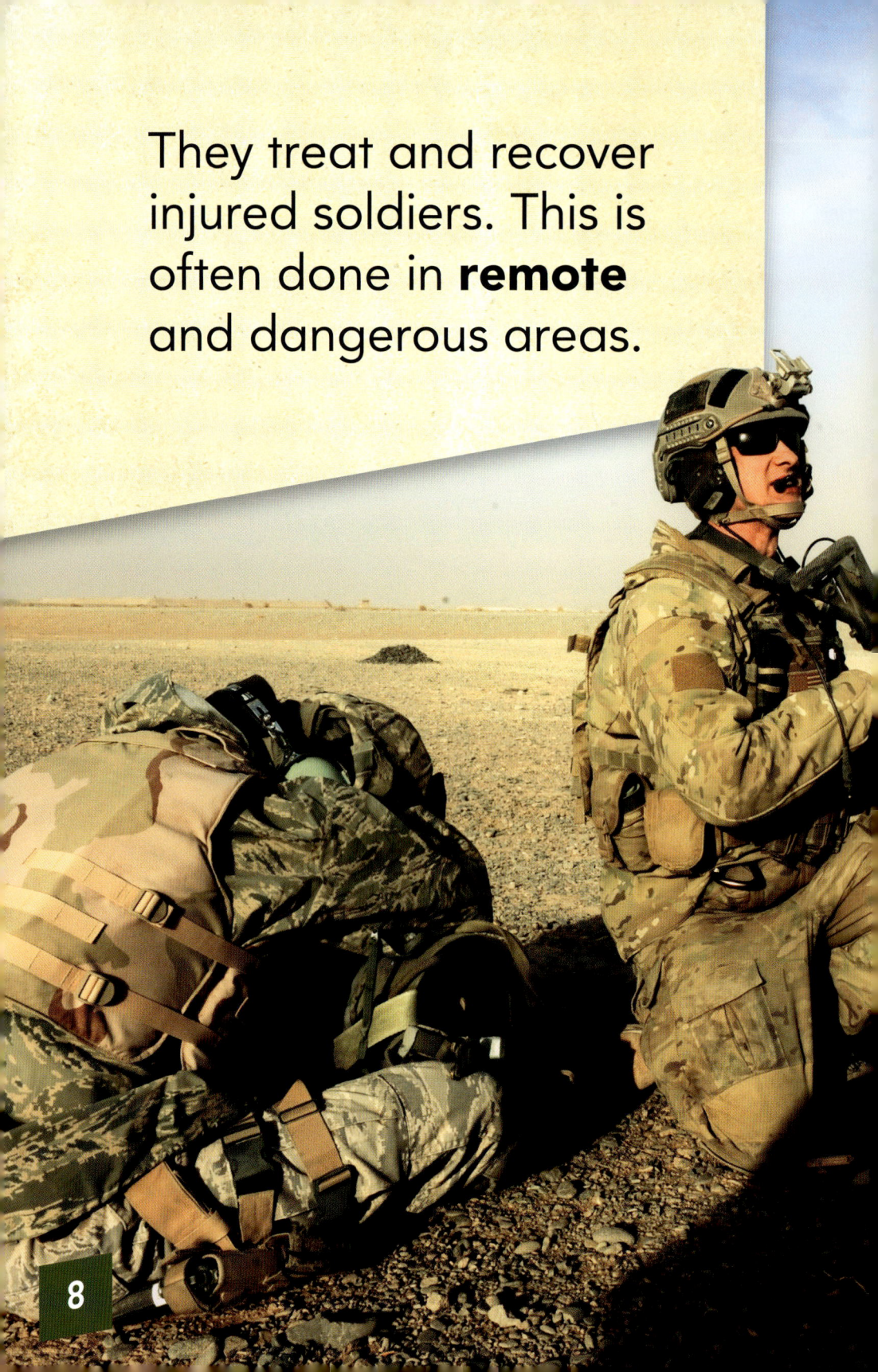

They treat and recover injured soldiers. This is often done in **remote** and dangerous areas.

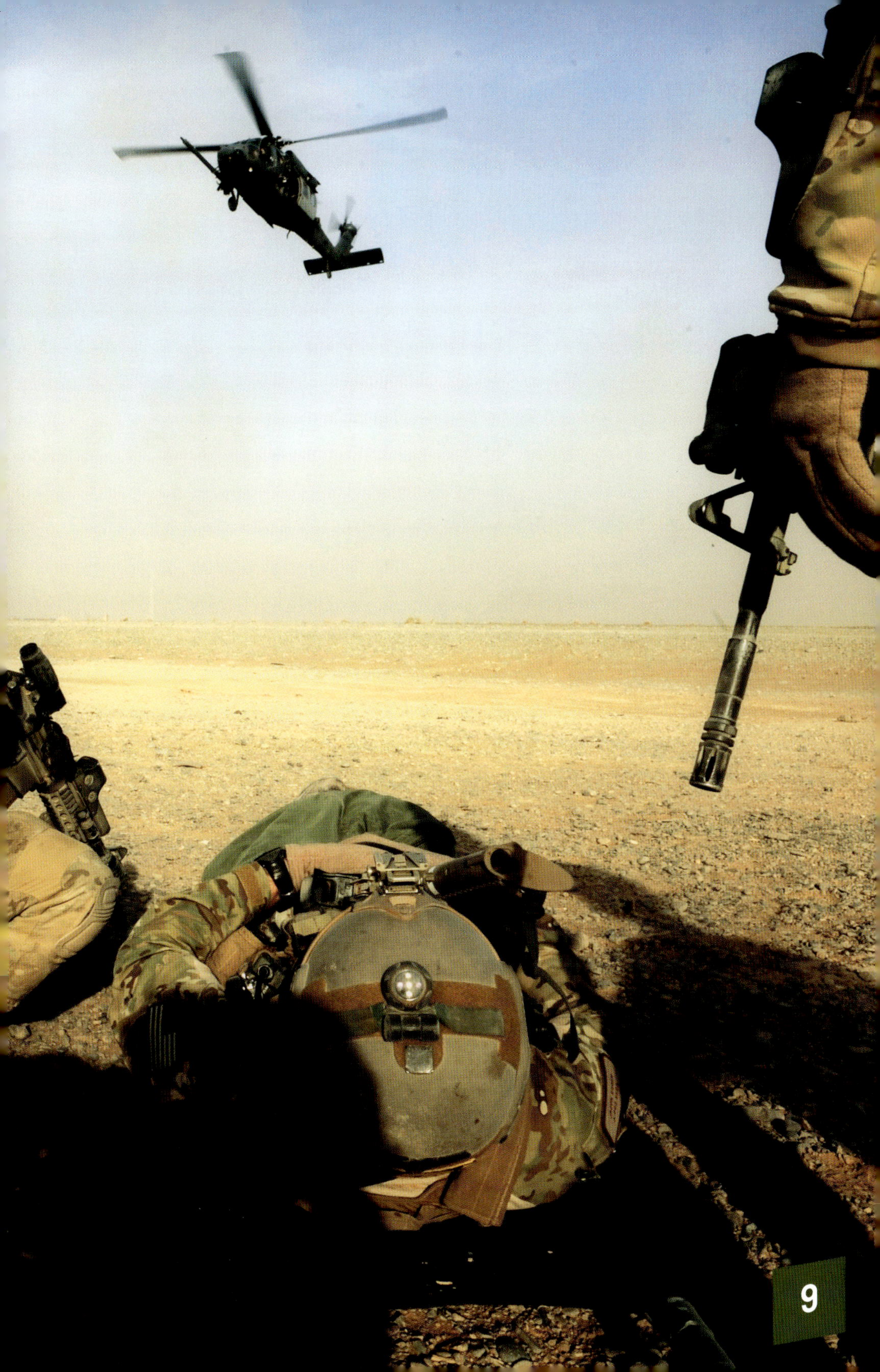

PJs help others too! In 2005, they rescued many people after Hurricane Katrina hit Florida and Louisiana.

11

Training

PJ training is tough. It lasts for two years. It is known as "Superman School."

13

14

PJs must pass physical tests. They learn to parachute, scuba dive, and rock climb!

PJs are trained in emergency medicine. They must be calm under pressure.

17

PJs are trained for all environments, including the Arctic and open water.

19

Today, more than 500 PJs are on **active duty**. They help save lives all over the world.

21

More Facts

- The United States **Air Force** Pararescue motto is, "These Things We Do, That Others May Live."

- PJs wear a maroon beret.

- Only 15-20% of those to attempt PJ training will complete it.

Glossary

active duty – a full-time occupation as part of a military force, as opposed to reserve duty.

Air Force – the branch of a nation's armed services that conducts military operations in the air.

remote – far from towns or human settlement.

Index

aircraft 6
Air Force 5
Arctic 18
equipment 6
Hurricane Katrina 10
medical treatment 8, 16

parachuting 6, 15
rescue 10, 20
rock climbing 15
scuba diving 15
training 12, 15, 18

Online Resources

Booklinks
NONFICTION NETWORK
FREE! ONLINE NONFICTION RESOURCES

To learn more about Air Force Pararescue, please visit **abdobooklinks.com** or scan this QR code. These links are routinely monitored and updated to provide the most current information available.